I0052941

ISO 37001

An Introduction to Anti-Bribery Management Systems

Doing the right things

ISO 37001

An Introduction to Anti-Bribery Management Systems

Doing the right things

ALAN FIELD

it gp ™

IT Governance Publishing

Every possible effort has been made to ensure that the information contained in this book is accurate at the time of going to press, and the publisher and the author cannot accept responsibility for any errors or omissions, however caused. Any opinions expressed in this book are those of the author, not the publisher. Websites identified are for reference only, not endorsement, and any website visits are at the reader's own risk. No responsibility for loss or damage occasioned to any person acting, or refraining from action, as a result of the material in this publication can be accepted by the publisher or the author.

Apart from any fair dealing for the purposes of research or private study, or criticism or review, as permitted under the Copyright, Designs and Patents Act 1988, this publication may only be reproduced, stored or transmitted, in any form, or by any means, with the prior permission in writing of the publisher or, in the case of reprographic reproduction, in accordance with the terms of licences issued by the Copyright Licensing Agency. Enquiries concerning reproduction outside those terms should be sent to the publisher at the following address:

IT Governance Publishing
IT Governance Limited
Unit 3, Clive Court
Bartholomew's Walk
Cambridgeshire Business Park
Ely, Cambridgeshire
CB7 4EA
United Kingdom
www.itgovernance.co.uk

© Alan Field 2017
The author has asserted the rights of the author under the Copyright, Designs and Patents Act, 1988, to be identified as the author of this work.

First published in the United Kingdom in 2017
by IT Governance Publishing.
ISBN 978-1-84928-953-5

ABOUT THE AUTHOR

Alan Field, MA, LL.B (Hons), PgC, MCQI CQP, MIIRSM, GIFireE, GradIOSH, is a chartered quality professional, an IRCA registered lead auditor and member of The Society of Authors.

Alan has particular expertise in auditing and third-party assessing anti-bribery management systems (ABMSs) to ISO 37001 and BS 10500 requirements, and counter-fraud systems in the public sector to ISO 9001 requirements. He has many years' experience with quality and integrated management systems in the legal, financial and property sectors. Alan also has experience in auditing, assessment and gap analysis roles within the project management sector.

CONTENTS

INTRODUCTION

What is ISO 37001:2016?

ISO 37001:2016 is the international standard for anti-bribery management systems (ABMSs) for organisations of all types and sizes, and in all parts of the world, that are committed to anti-bribery policies and controls.

The predecessor of ISO 37001 is BS 10500:2011. This, of course, is a British standard and although it attracted interest outside the UK, an international standard such as ISO 37001 will have a wider appeal across the globe.

ISO 37001 has a number of similarities to standards such as ISO 9001:2015, ISO 14001:2015 and ISO 27001:2013. This is because they all provide for a management system structured around ISO's Annex SL. Those organisations operating to, say, ISO 9001:2015 will find a wide degree of compatibility with the new ISO 37001:2016 in terms of broad approach and structure, e.g. a leadership-based, risk-based and process-based management system.

However, there are surprisingly few differences in terms of operational requirements between BS 10500:2011 and ISO 37001:2016 if the above structural changes are understood and implemented.

In short, ISO 37001 specifies a number of anti-bribery policies and procedures that an organisation can establish, implement and maintain in order to prevent bribery from occurring, and to help it to effectively identify and deal with any bribery that does occur.

What does ISO 37001 mean in terms of corporate policy?

An ABMS provides a framework for top management and other leadership elements of an organisation to decide upon risk-based objectives in order to minimise the risk of bribery impacting their organisation.

As with all management systems, it starts with leadership. An ABMS shows that an organisation is serious about legal compliance and that it is doing all it reasonably can to prevent itself from becoming involved in corrupt practices. It presents an ongoing commitment to continual improvement.

Implementing an ABMS helps organisations to mitigate reputational risk. Normally, the greater the public profile of an organisation, the more it needs to avoid being associated with anything that might be seen to be questionable by the law, regulators, its customers or any other stakeholders.

Having an ABMS in place does not guarantee compliance with ISO 37001, as an organisation still needs to adapt its culture, ensuring its commitment to anti-bribery is communicated throughout the business and well-practised. Implementing ISO 37001 helps organisations to promote and maintain a compliance approach to anti-bribery standards and laws, while ensuring that the ABMS is appropriate to the size of the organisation and the level of bribery risk it faces.

Risk-based approach to management

ISO 37001 follows the structure of Annex SL, which is an ISO document established as the framework for new assessable standards and revisions to existing ones (such as ISO 9001, ISO 14001 and ISO 27001).

One key element of Annex SL is that process-based management systems should define objectives in accordance with the organisation's risks and opportunities, whereby the leadership of the organisation decides the key risks and opportunities relevant to the management system.

The five main differences between ISO 37001 and its predecessor, BS 10500, are, broadly:

1. A new focus on leadership, through top management and the leadership of the governing body for the ABMS. The

term 'governing body' needs to be defined in your own organisation. Governance sits above the operational decision making of top management. The following list is not exhaustive, but in the public sector governance might be elected representatives, in a charity it might be its trustees, in a company it might be non-executive directors and/or an external regulatory body, and in a very large group of companies it might be the holding company's board of directors (supervising the board of its subsidiary).

2. There is no compliance manager requirement in ISO 37001 (unlike BS 10500). The ABMS is the direct responsibility of top management. However, top management may delegate some aspects of ABMS delivery to what ISO 37001 describes as the anti-bribery compliance function and, in some organisations, this may be a compliance manager.

3. The introduction of a risk-based approach to process management. This includes a requirement to plan and address actions to tackle risks and opportunities. This is also likely to feed into another new requirement, which includes defining the context of the organisation. One way of looking at this is to consider the overall ABMS risk created by the risk universe that the organisation operates in – leadership, staff, customers, suppliers, competitors, regulators, trade bodies and others – which in turn influences the risks and opportunities that will be defined.

4. More control over the anti-bribery approaches taken by business associates and any outsourced activity.

5. There is now a specific duty to manage inadequacy in anti-bribery controls. This was implied in BS 10500, but under ISO 37001, top management needs to take formal action. For example, if during a project the initial controls put into place to prevent bribery are not effective, leadership might have to withdraw from the project or any future projects with a corrupt party. It would certainly lead to a formal review of risk-based controls and due diligence generally.

Other points of interest:

- ISO 37001 has already formally replaced BS 10500 but a number of organisations are still using the latter and being assessed against it. The transition to ISO 37001 will take place over the coming months and new entrants are likely to adopt the Standard.
- Since ISO 37001 is based on Annex SL, ISO 37001 can be combined or integrated with other Annex SL-aligned management systems. Therefore, a number of processes – such as defining risks and conducting management reviews or internal audits – can be integrated into one suite of processes.
- The processes for defining the context of the organisation and defining the interests of stakeholders is similar to that in other Annex SL standards. However, with ISO 37001, these high-level analyses of the organisation and those it interacts with will feed into strategic decision making about the ABMS policy and the specific expectations of ISO 37001, such as the adequacy of anti-bribery controls.
- Some ISO 37001 requirements align with existing business processes. For example, the requirements relating to financial controls (clause 8.3), non-financial controls (clause 8.4) and anti-bribery commitments (clause 8.6) should only need some adjustments to existing contractual arrangements.
- Appendix A to ISO 37001 provides guidance notes to help further understand the above points.

CHAPTER 1: NO OSTRICHES ALLOWED: AN OVERVIEW OF ANTI-BRIBERY

The purpose of this guide is to provide guidance on implementing a management system to the requirements of ISO 37001:2016, the international standard relating to an ABMS. This will apply whether you are considering formal assessment or not.

Each ABMS will be as unique as any organisation's culture and circumstances. This guide will focus on the key areas that may need particular consideration and it will highlight other areas that may need further research.

It is also important that you read and consider the exact requirements of ISO 37001 in detail.

In the context of this publication, a management system is a framework where processes and/or procedures are used to ensure that tasks are delivered in a consistent way by an organisation to ensure its objectives are achieved.

Anti-bribery – although it may be a separate management system – may also be incorporated into many other aspects of compliance, ICT and HR policies, to name but a few. This will be examined further throughout the guide.

Ostriches and risk takers

Why consider ISO 37001:2016 at all?

The following scenario may not apply to your organisation, but the risks and assumptions it raises helps one consider the landscape that ISO 37001 seeks to manage.

You might call this scenario the ostrich approach to bribery and corruption risks: the belief that it will never happen in your organisation, and none of your customers, suppliers or contractors – or individual members of their staff – would ever engage in such practices. Many organisations still implicitly or even openly believe this. This might be because they simply see it as a very low risk, or because they prefer not to think that those they trust would abuse that relationship.

There may also be a fundamental misunderstanding in that just because an organisation itself is ethical and compliant in most respects, this does not necessarily prevent certain individuals working for them (and sometimes very senior individuals) from being corrupt. We will explore this distinction when we look at due diligence.

It is also sometimes forgotten that the links between corruption and fraud are very close. If an organisation has a counter-fraud policy with systems and controls in place, then there should be a similar process in place for bribery and corruption.

For example, if a subcontractor deliberately invoices a company for work they have not done, then that is probably fraud. If they tell one of the company's employees in advance and offer them an inducement to approve the invoice for payment, then that is corruption as well. To recognise one of these circumstance as a risk to be controlled but not the other, does not make good business sense.

Another example is where very large contracts can be won or lost based on relationships with clients, and where a 'beauty parade' system operates. There may actually be little or no difference in price or product quality between competitors for high-value contracts. Some organisations may give inducements to potential customers or their agents to get the order, which in some parts of the world is normal business practice. Some individuals may even believe they are doing nothing wrong, especially if these inducements are payments to 'charities' or trade bodies (which the client or agent will either be a direct beneficiary of or, perhaps, where a family member or other associates will benefit).

In the industrialised world, inducements may be presents instead of cash: holidays, lavish entertainment (including for family members), interest-free or low-interest loans, paying healthcare costs, paying other bills out of company funds, or rather more complex arrangements such as secret offshore investments.

1: No Ostriches Allowed: An Overview of Anti-Bribery

Although bribery may not be legal in any part of the world, its definition and how little it is enforced means that in some countries there is simply a lack of expectation for all parties to act honestly.

Some organisations take risks just by saying there is no risk at all: there is no bribery and corruption here – it only happens elsewhere. Others take the view that bribery and corruption only ever happen in the developing world and not in, say, the UK or US. They confuse the difference between risk and frequency. Bribery and corruption can happen anywhere – it is just more prevalent in some countries and in some business sectors.

One way to discourage dishonesty is to have rigorous processes and risk-based decision making, such as a check on the identities, qualifications and employment references of all new staff, no matter how senior or how well known they may be to managers or investors.

Some fraudsters and corrupt individuals may develop 'friendships' that are beneficial to them, even taking pleasure in manipulating senior business people into believing they are something they are not. The truth is that 'grooming' isn't just something done by sexual predators – deception is a common strategy used by many criminals. Few executives would ever admit they could fall victim to a con artist, but they could. An organisation needs to accept that this risk exists and put in place appropriate countermeasures.

The reasons for dishonesty are many and sometimes employees will become involved in criminality that is out of their previous character. This is even before we consider those business people who see nothing wrong in corrupt behaviour. Rigorous processes for checking candidates' backgrounds can minimise the risks.

This guide will discuss these points and others in more detail to give you a grounding in ISO 37001.

CHAPTER 2: AN ABMS BY ANY OTHER NAME

What is an ABMS?

An ABMS is not the same as financial and corporate governance rules to prevent bribery and fraud., but it can be integrated as a part of it. For organisations in the UK, corporate governance or financial controls should already be in place to meet the requirements of the Bribery Act 2010. However, implementing an ABMS – as understood by ISO 37001 – is still optional.

ISO 37001 is the new basis for most ABMS implementations. It is similar in approach to other international standards, such as ISO 9001:2015 (quality management systems) or ISO 14001:2015 (environmental management systems), in that it is based on a plan, do, check, act (PDCA) approach to decision making.

A PDCA approach can be generic and can influence the way other systems or processes within an organisation are developed. ISO 37001 can be integrated with other related PDCA-based management systems, such as ISO 9001.

In the UK, the Bribery Act 2010 is one of the key pieces of legislation. ISO 37001 can be adapted for other jurisdictions, as many of the general legal principles are similar. Because an ABMS is a management system, we can also adapt it to most legal or compliance systems. This is important if an organisation works in a number of different countries and decisions on specific issues need to comply with differing local, legal expectations.

If an organisation has a global approach to business ethics or corporate social responsibility, it should either be integrated into the ABMS or run in tandem. Where compliance and ethics run in different directions then, at the very least, mixed messages will be sent to staff.

Reinventing the wheel?

We will be using ISO 37001 as a guiding point for subsequent chapters but, equally, it will be useful for more compliance-based approaches, even for organisations that do not intend to formally implement ISO 37001.

When implementing an ABMS you are unlikely to be starting from a completely blank slate. Even a cursory read through ISO 37001 highlights lots of familiar things, including HR and procurement policies. Some of these policies may already be in place and meet ISO 37001, whereas others will need work and some requirements will be new. You should conduct a gap analysis to identify the difference between what you have and what you will need.

The following chapters will take you through the key requirements of ISO 37001, but we will look first at the areas where a gap analysis might find some quick wins.

There may already be a business ethics policy in place. If not, this is one of the first areas for top management to focus on. Implementing an ABMS, let alone being assessed against ISO 37001, is something the organisation has to be committed to. Such phrases are often written in management textbooks but this has to be more than an aspiration – an ABMS might be business as usual to some organisations but a fundamental shift to others. This is something to discover at the outset of an ABMS implementation and not halfway through.

The quick wins might fall into the following four areas:

1. Policy – if there is a developed corporate governance and compliance system in place, and/or a system of corporate social responsibility (sometimes known as corporate responsibility (CR)), then some of the policy and objectives requirements may already be present.

2. Documents and records – if you already have ISO 9001:2015 or a similar risk based management system in place, at least some of the document and data control systems will exist. IT Governance Publishing also

publishes an ISO 37001 toolkit that has standard forms and documents to help you.

3. Gifts and hospitality – if there are well-developed treasury controls over the payment and authorisation of business expenses, then this is a good start towards controlling gifts and hospitality processes. Many organisations already record or log gifts and hospitality, either received and/or given. In this case, the system might only need simple enhancements.

    Sometimes the stumbling block may be that such systems do not apply to directors and the most senior staff. Again, the cultural barrier needs to be broken down for everyone to accept that even the most senior, trusted individuals might be, or become, corrupt, even if the possibility is seen as highly remote. Where executive-level hospitality is being given or received there should always be some business justification for the time and resources used: is a legitimate business gain or opportunity being progressed that will more than return the expenditure? Or is it just an informal perk or jolly that is being exploited? Remember, there is never a free visit to an exotic location – somebody's shareholders (and possibly some country's taxpayers) are losing out to meet the cost. Even if executives have some discretion to incur expenses appropriate to their status and role, these should still be properly recorded and fully justifiable, with a non-corrupt motive. If the organisation has difficulty in understanding this, then it may struggle with implementing any type of ABMS.

    Some might argue that executive turkeys never vote for Christmas, but gifts and hospitality policies is one area where top management do need to lead from the top – stable, sustainable and ethical approaches to business are important and an ABMS has to acknowledge this.

4. HR processes – ISO 37001 assumes that an organisation needs to risk assess new staff and decide if, for example, they could present unacceptable probity risks or risks that

need specific controls. Although shady pasts may influence the decision, this is not the key determinant. For example, those whose roles involve little or no discretion in decision making may have a comparatively low bribery risk, which contrasts with a customs official making a decision about releasing a consignment, or a senior director approving a new contractor – they both have a high degree of discretion, despite their different levels of seniority. In other words, the job role and the probity risk it entails need to be examined.

There are also the practical circumstances. Some individuals – or some parts of the world that they will need to work in – may present blackmail or entrapment risks: that is, taking part in corrupt practices is not always a voluntary act.

ISO 37001 compliance involves following a number of pre- and post-employment practices, which include the vetting of candidates. This is usually interpreted as including processes such as checking candidates' identities, always getting references, and checking the validity of a candidate's qualifications and professional memberships.

A bribery risk area may involve the revolving door, where a person is rewarded with a position in the organisation after they (or a family member) have provided some service or favour. This not only highlights the different forms bribery can take but also underscores the importance of checking the background of new hires (and existing employees) for potential conflicts of interest, especially if they (or their relations) have had past or present dealings with your organisation.

The way that new employee (and especially director-level) packages are structured needs to be considered in terms of corruption risks. For example, payment of excessive commissions may not only reward high performance but also incentivise corruption. Keep this in mind when structuring compensation schemes or monitoring employees who are personally benefiting from achieving certain results.

Even some large organisations may be inconsistent in following the above points. These points don't just relate to probity. There are serious legal consequences for employing an individual who has no right to work in the UK, as well as the commercial consequences of employing someone without the qualifications they claim to have – civil engineering is just one example other than medicine where a licence to kill may be handed to someone. However, if an organisation does all or most of what ISO 37001 requires concerning HR processes, then this will greatly help in implementing the ABMS.

Taking into account these four points, reinventing the wheel may not be necessary for an ABMS. There may be a lot of synergy with the management systems already in place.

CHAPTER 3: MANAGEMENT PROCESSES WITHIN AN ABMS

Top dogs?

This is one of the shortest but, in many respects, the most important chapter. It is about how top and other senior management are involved with the ABMS.

Since ISO 37001 is a PDCA-based management system, the concepts of management responsibility are embedded and are very similar to those of ISO 9001. There are a few differences, however, and this chapter will explain the ISO 37001 concepts.

Top management

In ISO 37001, the chief role of top management is to conduct the management review of the ABMS (clause 5.3). They set the tone of the whole ABMS. The top manager may be an individual or a collective of senior management.

Top management should also agree and support the promulgation of the ABMS policy and the compliance declaration, agreeing to follow ethical conduct and ISO 37001. Top management needs to agree to follow these as the starting point for a successful ABMS.

Top management may also have a role in championing the need to have employment and procurement contracts that meet ABMS requirements.

An ABMS is not lip service or something that middle management gives the top manager to sign. It is – and needs to be seen as – a key part of strategic and compliance policy.

Leadership

One big change between BS 10500 and ISO 37001 is that there is no longer a compliance officer but instead the organisation's top management holds this role with appropriate delegation.

Unlike, say, ISO 9001:2015, leadership is explicitly a governing body that could be sitting above or alongside top management. Each organisation needs to decide what governance or a 'governing body' is within its leadership and strategic direction in terms of anti-bribery.

This governing body could be non-executive directors, the board of a holding company, a regulator or the rest of the leadership team.

Although it is still early days to be certain what assessment bodies will require in individual instances, governance is a broad term. Like the subtitle of this book, governance is making sure the right things are done, whereas top management ensures things are done right. What governance, top management and leadership mean in terms of anti-bribery need to be decided and defined at an early stage within an ABMS implementation.

The old compliance manager role required by BS 10500 may still continue in many organisations but accountability for these processes is now very much with top management. The compliance manager may be one individual but in large organisations they often have a deputy or team to assist them. They oversee implementation, development and compliance with the ABMS, and are often involved with training, internal audit and internal-investigation management.

The compliance manager will report to top management and should have direct access to them on any issue covered by ISO 37001, including investigations. This might include the CEO, or even the board or audit committee, depending on the size of the organisation. Remember ISO 37001 is run by top management so, in effect, any compliance manager would be an internal adviser/facilitator insofar as ISO 37001 is concerned.

The compliance manager should be able to raise concerns or questions directly with top management. This may not be with the chief executive but with a member of the corporate governance body, such as the chairman or a non-executive director, to ensure greater independence.

The management review process itself, which will be familiar to those who have dealt with management systems such as ISO 27001 and ISO 9001, will set and review policy, and look at all outputs from the ABMS, including the risk based approach to the ABMS. These might include soft and hard metrics on how the ABMS is operating, as well as considering continual improvement goals. The compliance manager's input should influence these deliberations and decisions.

The compliance function may also be involved in ensuring the appropriate training of staff and that the compliance declaration is understood and signed by all, as well as handling queries about the ABMS in practice. These might include queries on gifts and hospitality policy.

The compliance function will typically be involved with the due diligence and risk assessment process, although in large organisations this may be a shared role.

Other roles

A number of managers need to be involved with the ABMS and almost certainly engage with the compliance function regularly.

Each organisation is different in size, purpose and culture. The examples given illustrate how cross-functional activities or process responsibilities can affect an ABMS.

Examples include the chief financial officer, or their direct report responsible for treasury and financial audit issues. This may involve the company secretary, or others responsible for corporate governance.

The HR director, and the directors responsible for procurement and the selection of sub-consultants, also need to be involved, as may the manager responsible for quality, as well as health and safety, especially if an integrated management system is in place with an ABMS as an element of it. People responsible for overall regulatory compliance, including acquiring and maintaining necessary permits and licences, should involve the ABMS in their operations, just as those getting new business must.

The manager responsible for IT security will need to be consulted and, in some organisations with overseas operations, may also wish to consult with their security manager to align personal safety policies with the ABMS. In some organisations this may all be done by top management direct.

Staff

All staff need to follow the ABMS. It should become a part of business as usual – not just some compliance-driven bolt-on. This may involve optional or mandatory employee anti-bribery training (ahead of signing a compliance declaration). An ABMS is an integral part of the day-to-day management system, and virtually every manager concerned with risk or asset management should be aware of it and promoting it.

CHAPTER 4: IMPLEMENTING AN ABMS: ONE KEY ISSUE

What's a gift?

When implementing an ABMS, a gifts and hospitality policy is one of the most discussed and contentious areas to roll out to all staff.

If this can be done successfully, many of the other areas of the ABMS will be comparatively plain sailing.

Gifts may be cash, other items, services or activities of value. Value will be relative to the organisation, wider cultural perceptions in the country concerned and the purpose of the gift. A promotional biro with a logo on it is almost certainly not a bribe, whereas a sports car would be. The difficulty resides with items in between the two extremes and the circumstances in which they are offered or accepted.

Hospitality can merge into the concept of gifts, e.g. a relatively inexpensive meal to discuss a business prospect may be different to a lavish meal at a top hotel, and may be treated as such by a recipient, even if there was no corrupt intention. Business trips that merge into holidays, or even business trips that become a vehicle to offer gifts, including personal services, can become problematic unless there is a clear, well-communicated policy.

For example, an expenses-paid visit to a sporting event may be an inducement but if it is part of a wider, well-publicised marketing activity by an organisation, then it may not be. It all depends on circumstances. It should be risk assessed and also be subject to a gifts and hospitality policy agreed and championed by top management.

Top management also needs to champion the ethos that an ethical approach to business is vital. The gifts and hospitality policy is a key part of the 'shop window' of this policy in action.

Brutal truths have to be accepted by an organisation because denial is likely to come back and bite it later in the ABMS implementation.

1. Giving or accepting a bribe is unethical and illegal. Gifts and hospitality can be bribes irrespective of what customers may suggest otherwise. All staff and self-employed consultants need to understand and agree to this.
2. Appropriate and reasonable gifts or hospitality, properly recorded and authorised, are fine so long as the costs incurred are proportionate and reasonable (which need to be defined and risk assessed in each circumstance). It is also fine if the expenditure given or received is part of a duly authorised and properly accounted for marketing or promotional budget.
3. Senior staff shouldn't see gifts and hospitality budgets as a perk of their package. Although taking the chief executive of your largest client to a good restaurant might be appropriate, the same criteria apply: is the cost reasonable, proportionate and likely to be recoverable in increased profit or surplus, and will it be properly recorded and reported?
4. This rule especially applies where the award of a contract is restricted to a limited shortlist of equally balanced contenders, based on the decision of one person (or a very small group of individuals). Any gifts and hospitality given or received in such circumstances have to be very carefully considered and fully recorded at the time.
5. Even if a customer is blue chip this doesn't necessarily reduce the risk that much. They might still – unwittingly – be employing a corrupt individual. If that individual is ever caught, they may allege that it was you who initiated their dishonesty – known by lawyers as 'the cut throat' defence. Even people you thought were your friends in business may well be tempted to do this to protect their reputation and job or avoid imprisonment.

This risk alone justifies why there needs to be ABMS policies, procedures and good, consistent record keeping. Any ethical grey areas should always be referred to line or compliance management, because keeping things close to your chest can be seriously misconstrued at a later date.

If a gap analysis has been undertaken between ISO 37001 and the existing governance and treasury processes, it may be found that staff expense claims are already effectively managed and reported upon.

If there is a different approach to gifts and hospitality for senior staff, then this needs to be carefully defined. There should be an explicit policy decision about controls to be put in place for such an approach. This is one area where the 'governing body' requirement of ISO 37001 can offer a level of control.

In other words, this kind of policy needs to be planned and accepted by top management and leadership. An 'expense account' culture has to be risk managed on an ongoing basis and operated within the law.

ISO 37001 talks about charitable or political donations. This might be for legitimate business reasons, e.g. as part of a corporate social responsibility policy, part of duly authorised marketing or promotional activities, or to encourage team building among staff. All such donations (whether in time or money) should always be scrutinised by top management.

Where a branch office can make a cash or labour contribution to charity, then this should be authorised and risk assessed.

This is because small or newly established charities can be used as vehicles for fraud. There should be agreed due diligence, including whether any local staff may have a financial connection with the charity concerned, e.g. they act as a trustee or paid consultant.

In the developing world, charitable contributions may be a direct front for bribery, typically where local decision makers or their family members are beneficiaries to these funds. Even where it is not immediately apparent that an individual is directly connected to a charitable organisation, a strategic donation to their preferred cause or team may be made with the corrupt intent of influencing them. This is a form of bribery, just as if they were paid directly and then donated the money themselves.

Due diligence should look into the underlying philanthropic motivations of the actions and scrutinise how or why a particular cause was selected to be supported. For example, if a local official who has some discretionary authority over your business operations is the one who suggests supporting a community development initiative, then that should raise a red flag for further investigation.

On the record

If an organisation decides to adopt a 'no hospitality given or received' approach, this needs to be communicated to customers to ensure no offence or other issues are created. This should not be left to junior management. There should be a clear, consistent message from top management. If this is not planned, different layers of management may give different messages or even encourage different operational practices among customers.

If a controlled approach to gifts and hospitality is decided upon, limits of acceptability need to be set and briefed to staff. This may be monetary, such as a percentage of salary, or by specific limitations, e.g. a sandwich lunch is permitted but no alcohol. Exceptions for sales staff or senior managers also need to be defined. Top management need to show accountability for any issues, even if tactical decisions are left to HR or Finance to manage.

Gifts and hospitality received need to be fully recorded. There may be one central log or more local records kept, but there needs to be an agreed, regular approach to reviewing the log. Where trends are identified, a clear policy towards investigation is needed. All staff at all levels of the organisation need to understand that it is important to the business for compliance and wider reputational or marketing reasons.

Practical hospitality issues, such as attendance at sporting events or other potentially expensive activities, need to be considered a policy issue at an early stage. Different organisations will take different views about what is reasonable and proportionate, what their guiding principles are and whether corporate hospitality can be reciprocated. Transparency and consistency of decision making on such points is vital.

Some organisations will only invite multiple parties to such hospitality events, so it cannot be argued that one individual or organisation is solely benefiting. And some organisations will accept no hospitality whatsoever – not even a cup of coffee.

All approaches need to be risk managed – just because more than one customer's representative(s) are present doesn't necessarily mean the hospitality is for a legitimate business purpose. However, a proportionate approach to risk based thinking also needs to be considered – sometimes a cup of coffee is simply just that.

Gifts and hospitality can be lifecycle driven, e.g. what might be acceptable hospitality during normal business operations may not be so during a re-tendering process or a contractual or payment dispute between the parties.

If international business is undertaken, briefing and policies for each territory need to be agreed and implemented. In terms of a long-term business relationship, this can be time consuming if many different cultures and interests need to be considered, and parties consulted. This will be discussed further in the due diligence section.

Some organisations permit modest hospitality to be given or accepted without formally recording this. It should be decided if this still needs to be more informally reported, e.g. an email to line management. Both fraud and corruption tend to operate within secret arrangements and/or where controls are weak, so you should always err on the side of over-reporting. Although this might take some working time, it is essential to have all such transactions properly documented.

Remember that just reporting something doesn't make it legal or within policy, but it gives line management the opportunity to question it. The chapter on investigations will look at how apparent breaches of the policy should be progressed.

Top management needs to have agreed protocols for dealing with clients and key suppliers who have issues with understanding or accepting the organisation's policy. This will be discussed further in the due diligence chapter.

If all staff accept and understand the gifts and hospitality policy – and can operate it consistently – then your organisation is a long way towards implementing an ABMS.

CHAPTER 5: RISK ASSESSMENT IN DUE DILIGENCE

Risk assessment in relation to due diligence

As with any other compliance risk, there should be an agreed programme of risk assessments for the risks of bribery and corruption, including any perceived risk of blackmail or other forms of intimidation. This needs to be consistent with the risk- and opportunities-based approach required by ISO 37001. Due diligence may, in reality, be a suite of more tactical processes that sit below these high-level policies and controls.

Some risk assessments will be combined with others within the organisation, e.g. treasury or procurement controls and wider security assessments, especially if business activities are regularly undertaken in higher-risk sectors or countries.

This guide will highlight some specific areas of risk that an ABMS should consider.

Some organisations will go to great lengths to classify sectors and countries that may have higher risks than others. For example, the 'Corruption Perceptions Index'[1] is frequently used for guidance.

A number of law firms and other consultancies will provide information on different areas of the world, and credit reference and other financial information databases will provide details to help due diligence decision making.

Due diligence and facilitation payments

The due diligence requirements of ISO 37001 closely align with compliance and governance generally, especially procurement, credit controls and some aspects of treasury controls. Although

---

[1]

www.transparency.org/news/feature/corruption_perceptions_index_20 16 the ABMS may need a slightly wider reach, many organisations find that their existing systems are a good starting point.

Due diligence is a complex area and is dependent on individual circumstances. It might be seen as a risk assessment or probity assessment of a business associate. The definition of business associate is very wide in ISO 37001 and includes customers.

It is important to conduct due diligence on subcontractors, service providers and other consultants. This begins with understanding what they will be doing for you, and especially if they interact with government officials, ensuring they are not using improper means to attain outcomes. It is also advisable to have at least higher-risk (if not all) parties complete anti-bribery compliance forms and include anti-bribery provisions in your contracts with them.

Many organisations are comfortable with credit checking potential customers, but sometimes a cultural adjustment has to be made to the idea that they might turn down business simply because they see the customer as potentially unethical or demonstrating an unacceptable reputational risk.

In terms of all business associates, the level of risk will often be related to the sector and part of the world from where they operate, their own compliance history and the level of exposure for the organisation, e.g. there might be a higher degree of risk working with a joint venture partner than the occasional use of a contractor, unless the latter is involved in very high-risk activities. There should also be an ongoing process of revisiting these at a defined frequency set by the organisation.

Business associates that have a negligible business do not need to be formally reviewed. 'Negligible' needs to be defined by the organisation and what may be negligible in one context may not be in another, depending on the nature, scope and location of individual projects or other activities.

'Negligible' will also be based on the level of corruption risk for the process itself, e.g. a corruption risk related to awarding a contract. However, if the majority of the day-to-day relationships will not involve more junior staff in situations where corruption is a possibility (e.g. there are no financial transactions or other activities where junior employees need to exercise discretion or approval), then this impacts on what is deemed 'negligible'.

Candid appraisal is vital. Does the organisation deal with any customer, contractor or other associate if the price is right? If the answer is 'yes', then a lot of strategic planning and cultural alignment will be needed. If ethical and reputational issues are carefully considered with any business, including customers, then there may be little more to do to meet due diligence requirements.

For example, even if a business associate is seen as blue chip or a public entity, this does not automatically make them have a low probity risk. They may – unwittingly – be employing a corrupt individual or team and, in the private sector, a business recently acquired by the blue chip company may not yet be operating to the probity standards they imagine.

Reputational risks and loss of market need to be given the same priority as legal compliance risks. The attitude of shareholders (or other stakeholders) to reputational damage or legal liability can be powerful drivers to moving forward with a due diligence process.

The roles and responsibilities for decision making need to be defined. The greater the risk and more potentially serious the outcome, the greater the seniority that should be involved with due diligence decisions. This is especially true where high-value business or other relationships could be compromised by a less than ethical approach.

Facilitation payments

Facilitation payments are illegal even if they are made on the organisation's behalf by third parties. The fact that the arrangement may be lawful in the local market is not a justification. This needs to be clearly understood by all staff.

Top management needs to give clear policy guidance about what to do if there is a query as to whether a particular arrangement or payment is considered legitimate. Of course, introduction fees and agents' commissions can be legitimate – circumstances and proportionality should form part of the due diligence process. Remember that the term 'payment' here includes indirect payments or inducements.

Facilitation payments can involve public officials and business associates agreeing to do things more quickly or differently in return for cash or other inducements.

Facilitation payments in some parts of the world can be closely aligned to blackmail or intimidation, e.g. there are physical threats if the request for a facilitation payment is refused. Blackmail may concern personal or professional indiscretions involving a member of staff that a customer, contractor or public official then uses to get favourable decisions to their financial benefit. This can happen anywhere but is surprisingly common in areas of high personal security risk, and the risk should be included as part of the staff security briefing.

In some parts of the world, facilitation payments may be masked as political or charitable donations, normally where the public official or customer (or their family) are an indirect beneficiary of the 'donations'. In the UK, there are occasional frauds involving purported 'charities', and there is always the risk that an employee, contractor or customer might gain a pecuniary benefit from these arrangements.

If the organisation operates abroad, or through a branch network where contractors or joint venture partners deal with public officials on its behalf, then it needs to have equally thorough controls to prevent facilitation payments. Management should never turn a blind eye to facilitation payments that are made on their behalf, perhaps being processed as additional consultants' fees or expenses.

The only exception is where threats have been made against staff and their security cannot be guaranteed unless a payment is made before their removal from the territory concerned; however, this would be a one-off event and might even lead to the project/service not proceeding.

Under ISO 37001 there is a specific requirement to manage the inadequacy of anti-bribery controls and this could be one example where the process would be invoked. The aim is not just better due diligence in future but continual improvement generated through these insights and controls.

A practical example of due diligence management

All invoices from contractors and joint venture partners should be checked to ensure fees and expenses are reasonable, justified and were actually incurred. This will minimise the risk of any inappropriate payments being hidden as other expenditure, such as facilitation payments made on the organisation's behalf. Any existing counter-fraud policies may have a bearing on this too.

With project and branch office-related work, one control is to give a contractor a budget, so if invoices go off budget, this will generate a query. Another control would be to ensure that contractor invoices have to be approved by more than one person for payment, no matter how senior they may be, which minimises the risk of fraud and corruption.

Conclusion

Due diligence can have significant commercial consequences. Nobody likes turning profitable business away or breaking relationships with valued agents or contractors. Yet an ethical approach to business is not just a legal obligation but a way to protect reputation and business growth.

CHAPTER 6: WHO DO YOU THINK THEY ARE?

What is an ABMS?

An ABMS can help an organisation achieve accurate information on the people employed in the organisation, from the most senior to the most junior.

ISO 37001 assumes that an organisation risk assesses new staff and new roles, including how documentation is used to help achieve this goal. Even if fully attaining ISO 37001 is not a goal, an ABMS needs to consider the processes in place to verify what may just be assumed about new staff.

The following example shows the implications behind an ABMS that can have a wider risk management perspective than just preventing bribes, and also indicates the importance of risk assessments within all aspects of an ABMS.

An organisation needs an approach to ensure all new staff can meet the requirements of ISO 37001. This is typically risk based. One way to minimise risk is to require that all new staff prove their identities. There has been much in the media about the 'hijacking' of identities, usually for financial crimes.

Other scams include individuals obtaining false identities, normally supported by a passport and other documents, and people owning more than one identity (the author has seen an individual with three concurrent identities for different business and personal aspects of their lives). One other option might be where an individual abuses the identities of those with a similar name, e.g. if another Alan Field is about my age and is a qualified doctor, then I might be able to get a job in a foreign hospital, purporting to be this other Alan Field, assuming I got hold of his necessary documentation or falsified it.

Many of these scams are operated and serviced by organised crime gangs. They may later use blackmail or inducements to get their 'customers' for these documents and services to commit criminal acts for them – and their current employer would be one likely victim. This could be a high risk to any current employer of that individual or their immediate family, e.g. an employee buying a false identity for a 'mail-order bride' so as to 'give' them an EC member state passport might then become the victim of blackmail.

The following pre- and post-employment practices should be adopted:

1. Checking passports or other identity documents, including NI numbers and tax codings (although an NI number may not be genuine). These checks might include making sure that all identity and qualification certificates show consistent spellings of the applicant's names, dates and place of birth. Inconsistencies should be queried.

    If you are not familiar with passports or other immigration documents for a particular country, then always check these out because a number of EC member states have been targeted by criminal gangs, either for excellent forgeries of the real thing, or documents that simply purport to be them (hoping that an employer won't know what the real thing looks like). Lost or stolen genuine passports may be doctored – one of the reasons for checking dates of birth and spelling of names on all documents. Fantasy or camouflage passports – legitimately offered for sale and then bought for novelty purposes or, supposedly, disguising one's true nationality from kidnappers or hijackers – may be presented as genuine immigration documents.

    For example, 'passports' for 'Netherlands Guiana' or 'Dutch Guiana' (broadly what is now Suriname today) might be presented to an employer with the suggestion that the person is a Dutch citizen. There are many other fantasy examples relating to names that might be broadly construed as being part of modern-day France or Germany.

    If you are not certain about a passport, always make enquiries. After all, the potential employee may even erroneously believe that they had been sold a 'genuine' EC citizenship. Therefore, in good faith, you will be told this with the same genuine honesty from that individual's perspective.

2. References should be checked and preferably obtained before the new staff member starts work. If the role involves any other security checks, e.g. CRB or credit reference checks, then the results should be compared with the information provided by referees. Unsatisfactory or inconclusive references should always be investigated.

    Where references cannot be obtained for whatever reason, alternative referees should be sought. References should be obtained for all new employees, even for senior roles or those who might be known to existing staff – false or multiple identities can be carried on for many years.

3. Check qualifications. A false CV or a genuine CV with exaggerations may be presented. Postgraduate or professional qualifications that are important to a role might be claimed that haven't been achieved, so insist on seeing the original certificates. Even better is to request the candidate to have the institution send a copy or other document confirming that the claimed credential is valid directly to you, without having the candidate as an intermediary as they could alter the documents. Many universities have forms for graduates to fill in that give consent to allow a potential employer to directly receive copies of degrees or academic transcripts. If you are not certain whether a university or college is recognised then this should be checked.

    Certificates from legitimate universities in troubled areas of the world – where making enquires may now be practically difficult – should be discussed with the new employee and perhaps with referees, to see if they checked the qualifications in more stable times.

    Some organisations also have a probationary period that is used to test whether the qualifications presented align with practical experience demonstrated. This should be flagged to the line management concerned. The author has seen several instances where line management have queried a new employee's CV after seeing their professional work in the first few months of employment. Such awareness from line management should be encouraged.

Arguably, none of the above points make a person more prone to bribery than another more honest individual, but they all help support sound risk management principles and an ABMS approach.

CHAPTER 7: BLOWING THE WHISTLE

ISO 37001 talks about raising concerns, or 'whistle-blowing' as it is more commonly known.

Whistle-blowing has been in the media recently, where it has been suggested that even when genuine concerns are reported, the whistle-blowers receive little or no thanks and may even face allegations themselves or are ostracised.

This guide cannot change the world but it does explain how an effective whistle-blowing process can be established. Whistle-blowing is like many aspects of an ABMS, where top management really do need to lead from the top. The organisational culture needs to be one where malpractice and wrongdoing are not accepted at any level.

Whistle-blowing is a much wider issue than bribery and corruption. For example, whistle-blowing often relates to HR and security issues: allegations of bullying and victimisation, allegations of misuse of company time, and allegations of fraud or theft of physical property. Similar allegations can also be made against contractors or customers' representatives.

Allegations might purely relate to non-adherence to internal procedures that have no external or legal bearing whatsoever.

Whistle-blowing can generate a mixed bag of investigative strands and there needs to be clear management responsibility for who investigates what. Investigations are covered in the next chapter.

Whistle-blowing processes have been with some organisations for a very long time. However, in the UK there was little or no legal need for them until the Bribery Act 2010 came into force, and the Ministry of Justice recommended that whistle-blowing hotlines be part of the 'adequate procedures' for protecting against bribery, outlined in Section 7 of the Bribery Act. This section introduced the offence of failure to prevent bribery. Businesses that either must follow or voluntarily accept the US

Sarbanes-Oxley requirements also need to have whistle-blowing hotlines. It is also a requirement of ISO 37001.

What is a hotline?

Initially, whistle-blowing is confidential to protect the whistle-blower, to protect the individuals(s) whom the allegations are being made against and to protect the reputation of the organisation itself. Confidentiality also protects any other stakeholders involved, including customers, from mistaken or malicious allegations. If the allegations relate to criminal activity, then further evidence may be needed, and the perpetrators should not be put on notice that their activities have been reported.

Most whistle-blowing hotlines will be telephone-based services but may also be web or email based. There are obvious data protection issues and a risk that individuals will be tipped off that allegations have been made against them. Some organisations would say that none of their senior staff would ever tip off friends in the organisation, but with an AMBS the concept of trust is different and needs to be seen as such.

In any event, those who receive the whistle-blower's information are at risk of suspicion if there were any subsequent leaks, even if they did not instigate them. Someone could also be whistle-blowing in the contractor's or customer's organisation, and if their investigations emerge at a later date then allegations of tip-offs might also arise from these external sources.

All these factors lead to why many organisations now use outside security or HR companies to manage their whistle-blowing hotlines, which only report to a few very senior individuals within the organisation. Sometimes the same company will carry out investigations directly or give advice on their ongoing management, especially if there is police involvement, or if contractors or customers need to be contacted. Sometimes a skilled outsider will manage the initial contacts better than those with much invested in the relationship already.

With ISO 37001, it is typically the compliance manager who is the point of contact with the security company, but it could be directly to the chairman or chief executive where there are allegations of fraud or bribery. With HR-related issues, such as allegations of bullying, these would probably go to the HR director in the first instance. However, all allegations should be fully examined and any patterns of conduct discerned.

For example, there may be an allegation of bullying that then develops into an allegation of, say, the individual suggesting that their line manager is bullying them because they have become aware of that manager's corrupt behaviour. There is a case to be made for ensuring that all allegations come into one central point until the full extent of any emerging issues are known.

As part of the management review process, trends and outcomes of whistle-blowing should be reported for data protection and confidentiality reasons, although ongoing investigations would not be discussed. The security company's reliability, service levels and consistency of ongoing advice should be monitored like any other contractor.

The issue of what should happen with whistle-blowers who make malicious or otherwise unfounded allegations is complex. If an organisation wants to avoid dealing with an issue, it is very simple to say the whistle-blower had an axe to grind or had a history of unsatisfactory performance.

Genuine misunderstandings can arise and, of course, at all levels of management there may be varying degrees of personal friction between direct reports and their line management, which may have coloured perceptions of events. Many organisations prefer to believe their own publicity material about being 'one big happy team' but it is not always as simple as that. To pretend otherwise is creating bigger problems at a later date.

The guiding principle should be to investigate the allegation first and then come to a determination, rather than to automatically believe or doubt the whistle-blower. If this isn't done, you end up investigating a whistle-blower before the allegation. The exception might be when a preliminary investigation suggests that the allegation has a different primary motivation.

A genuine whistle-blowing allegation should always be actioned. Whistle-blowing is sometimes about comparatively mundane issues.

Apparent dishonesty by contractor or customer representatives can be especially tricky to deal with. If you don't inform on your customer then it may be later alleged that you were colluding with them, which may mean police involvement. Whistle-blowing often means that proper legal advice has to be taken before deciding how to proceed.

If it is discovered that the allegation was malicious, then that is likely to be dealt with as a disciplinary matter.

Where an allegation was genuinely made but found to be without foundation or there was insufficient evidence, then that is more difficult. HR policy and individual circumstances may dictate what needs to be done. Mistrust between individuals is often indicative of interpersonal barriers or wider business challenges that need to be managed by the organisation. Being an ostrich on such matters could simply set up deeper challenges later.

ISO 37001 expects it to be a disciplinary offence to retaliate against someone who raises a concern in good faith.

This should be clearly outlined as part of your corporate ethics and whistle-blowing policy: whistle-blowers will not be retaliated against (not fired, demoted, receive a worse performance report, etc.) for truthfully reporting misconduct. Management must firmly adopt this philosophy towards whistle-blowers, who might otherwise be unpopular within the organisation.

Whistle-blowing can be a powerful, if unwelcome, tool in an organisation. Yet welcome it should be. Its purpose is to improve controls and show continual improvement – the organisation and its future are always bigger than individual miscreants who may be highlighted through the whistle-blowing process.

CHAPTER 8: INVESTIGATING BRIBERY

It is essential that the organisation's policies relating to investigation and consequences are fully understood before any ISO 37001 implementation is planned.

ISO 37001 requires that there are processes for investigating bribery or any weakness in the ABMS, and that appropriate action is taken if the investigation reveals bribery or any breach or weakness within the ABMS. This is a good starting point for any ABMS and, of course, these need to be risk based and proportionate.

Some organisations, particularly smaller ones, may have no formal investigation processes, so some consultancy help may be needed initially. Other organisations prefer to use specialist consultants for all such services. All decision making on the instigation and outcome of investigations needs to come from top management.

It is essential that the organisation's compliance policies about investigation and consequences are fully understood by all layers of management, and that there is a commitment to consistent application. One true test of an organisation's commitment to an ABMS is investigating someone who is commercially very important to the organisation. Where bribery is occurring it is likely that the perpetrators are just these individuals, ones who have been bringing in good results for the organisation (through their corrupt activities).

An investigation process that is just used to hasten the exit of staff seen as inefficient brings the legitimacy of the process into disrepute. This is an HR or commercial issue. It would also lead to real investigations becoming more difficult to conduct. Top management need to lead on this point and try to use a 'without fear or favour' policy with instigating an investigation.

The nuts and bolts

If there isn't already an agreed process for investigating bribery allegations, Finance may have one relating to counter-fraud investigations. The branch of accountancy involved in identifying vulnerabilities and managing outcomes from fraud is called forensic accountancy, and larger auditing firms have their own team to support clients.

Fraud is a very broad term that covers a number of crimes and other regulatory infringements. Risks of fraud might range from relatively minor abuses of staff travel and entertainment expense accounts, to organised and systematic corporate frauds that could impact the ongoing viability of the organisation. There is a direct link between bribery and fraud, especially where it is alleged that there has been collusion between a customer and/or contractor and a member of staff.

Some fraud falls within a broader definition of cyber crime, and those responsible for identifying vulnerabilities and investigating breaches of information security are often separate from those involved with forensic accountancy, although some organisations ensure there is a crossover.

HR departments usually have processes to investigate allegations of misconduct or other inappropriate behaviour in the workplace. This might include discrimination or bullying, which can have a direct bearing on fraud and bribery, e.g. where a supervisor coerces their direct reports to either cooperate with or keep silent about their own wrongdoing. There could be a direct link if a member of staff alleges that a corrupt line manager is trying to manage them out of the business due to what they know about the manager's improper activity. This could even be someone at board level.

If these investigative processes aren't in place, they need to be because there may be legal consequences for not looking at all these matters, e.g. a greater risk of prosecution under the Bribery Act 2010.

As with all business planning there needs to be a clear goal, or a set of outcomes expected from the investigation process.

These could include:

- Establishing if there are any local processes and procedures for investigation within the organisation, even if they are not called as such. Depending on the size and structure of the organisation, it may be necessary to consult the HR, IT, information security, finance and legal functions on these points. With smaller organisations they are likely to take legal advice at an early stage. If necessary, a gap analysis should be done across the organisation to see if there is any duplication or conflict.

- Deciding who will be responsible for managing investigations. Top management support is vital with bribery and fraud allegations. A very senior manager – possibly the chairman or a non-executive director – will be informed about all such allegations. They will also receive reports on the progress of investigations and personally agree to any external actions, such as hiring external investigators or involving the police.

- Decision making at top management level is important because there is a distinct possibility that the allegations may involve one or more senior members of staff or, perhaps, a high-profile consultant or subcontractor. Even if more senior individuals are not directly involved in the alleged scheme, they may have knowledge of it, or prefer to cover it up once it is brought to their attention. Without such controls, unsubstantiated allegations could be unfairly disseminated throughout the organisation and, equally, if there are guilty parties, then their allies could destroy evidence or covertly obstruct an investigation. Nobody likes to think of trusted colleagues doing such things but the risk exists.

- Where the organisation has a compliance manager (as required by ISO 37001), they will often be the point of preliminary investigation. This needs to be supported by top management. They supervise the investigations or delegate to others better qualified. A specialist consultant can be employed, e.g. a security, HR, legal or forensic accountancy specialist, depending on the circumstances, and they would normally report through the compliance manager, unless it were decided that they should report directly to top management or the board.

- Clear terms of engagement need to be agreed with either internal or external consultants. Investigations are potentially delicate and the investigator must be aware in advance of the approach to be taken and any limitations to their role the organisation wishes to impose. An external investigator needs to demonstrate competence and discretion. The slightest deviation from this standard should lead to termination of the contract.

- A predetermined policy needs to be agreed by top management about the outcome of investigations where wrongdoing is established. This might involve disciplinary action, dismissal or referral to the police. No matter how senior or valuable an employee may be, appropriate action must be taken.

- HR management will need to be consulted if there is the potential for disciplinary or other formal action against staff. A predetermined protocol needs to be established.

- If the findings of any investigations implicate a contractor or a customer, then specialist legal counsel will definitely need to be taken. There is the bigger risk of conspiracy allegations being made by prosecutors against the organisation at a later date, if it is felt a blind eye was turned to any third-party dishonesty.

Investigations are complex and may be new to a client. Yet an ABMS is important if procedures and policies are not in place for investigations.

One approach is always to treat investigations as not just being the teeth of the process but to identify new and emerging risks and the opportunity for continual improvement.

CHAPTER 9: INTERNAL AUDITING AND CORRECTIVE ACTION

An ABMS internal audit is an important part of ISO 37001, and those with existing management systems, such as ISO 9001 or ISO 27001, will be familiar with the concept.

Internal audit here is an entirely different concept from internal audit in a financial sense, and relates to testing whether the ABMS is meeting the requirements of ISO 37001 and the documented management system that supports it in the organisation concerned.

This chapter is an expanded version of some material in IT Governance Publishing's ISO 37001 Toolkit, which has a number of model forms to support the internal audit process discussed below.

1. Define an audit plan or schedule. The number of individual audits will depend on the size and complexity of the organisation, and whether one or two periods per year of intense auditing are preferred to smaller, monthly audits. Auditing planning should be risk based. Where audit plans are to be integrated or combined with, say, ISO 27001, there needs to be clear understanding on the part of both auditees and auditors that ABMS issues are also being examined.
2. Normally, the audit programme will be handled by the compliance function. If that is, say, the manager for ISO 9001 or ISO 27001, then they need to be sufficiently cross-trained to understand ISO 37001. This equally applies if a financial audit or governance manager is used to supervise the planning of ISO 37001 audits.
3. Auditors need to be competent in the requirements of ISO 37001. If a governance or HR specialist undertakes an audit, they need to be aware of the appropriate parts of ISO 37001.
4. Although all areas of ISO 37001 need to be covered over, say, a 12-month period, the actual frequency of an audit

needs to be determined based on the organisation's own ABMS. This is why there needs to be considerable thought given to a 12-month audit plan and certainly if a 24- or 36-month plan is preferred.

5. The audit plan needs to be dynamic because the results of audits might change the frequency or scope of later audits. Reports should never be filed without action.

Where the action is

Corrective actions are the next steps taken where risks or deficiencies are identified. Corrective action means that something does not conform to either ISO 37001 or the requirements of the ABMS. This is one reason why an ABMS shouldn't have inspirational elements: say what you do and prove what you do.

1. Decide how corrective actions will be styled. A certification body will typically use major and minor categories of nonconformities (NCs) – a major being a 'showstopper' where there is a complete breakdown or lack of evidence of compliance to a particular clause of ISO 37001 or part of the ABMS system. If internal audits follow the same approach, then how different NCs are communicated and actioned internally needs to be agreed in advance.

2. For all NCs a corrective action plan or programme will be agreed with the auditee. This will explain what will be done and by when to resolve the NC. The management review process should review all NCs and whether deadlines have been met. NCs may indicate a resolution that needs significant resource, which may need top management direction before anything is done.

3. Annex SL and the requirement under ISO 37001 to manage the inadequacy of anti-bribery controls mean that root cause analysis is important. Resolving the corrective action is not enough – the reason the nonconformity arose needs to be understood and action taken to prevent its reoccurrence. This is really another way of looking at the adequacy of risk-based controls. There are formal root

cause analysis concepts or tools that can be used by all manner of management systems.

4. If observations or other formally recorded comments are included in reports, it needs to be decided how these will be actioned: just a record of an auditee's observation for a future audit trail, or a minor issue that will need resolution in due course. If it is the latter, then there will need to be a tracking system, which some organisations include on a corrective action register or similar record.

Conclusions

The ABMS internal audit process needs careful planning. The correlation with financial and other governance auditing can either test one and other findings or, more likely, define the discreet elements of a system that different members of the audit team will sample.

There also needs to be careful alignment between the way NCs or other formal outcomes are recorded from different audits and then actioned in a coordinated way.

Also consider the way audits align with the investigation process. Although the vast majority of ABMS audits will not generate forensic enquiries, a protocol should be in place.

Internal audit should be a positive process. An ideal scenario is where audit becomes part of the continual improvement mechanism, rather than simply a mechanism for inspection and checking.

CHAPTER 10: GOING FOR GOLD

This final chapter considers the pros and cons of certification to ISO 37001 and the process itself. Is it worth doing?

If an organisation already has, say, ISO 9001, then the process of external assessment to achieve ISO 37001 will be clear.

Implementing an ABMS that meets the requirements of ISO 37001 is a goal in itself. The desire to be externally assessed shouldn't be seen as an obligation but a specific goal in itself.

The key determinant with any assessment product is to decide why you want it. Some organisations believe that without external assessment they would not progress with continual improvement to the same degree. The other extreme would be to decide that you want a certificate simply to prove compliance with the Standard. Drifting into assessment is not worth considering because, as well as management commitment, there are the even greater ongoing commitments of time and resources to maintain it.

ISO 37001 is a PDCA-based system. Although it can be aligned with compliance processes, achieving ISO 37001 certification proves something more than just saying that you have a fully compliant system – it is saying that you have a management system in place that supports ongoing compliance. Depending on the organisation's culture, that might be more challenging than proving mere compliance.

Beware of consultants or assessment bodies persuading you to have ISO 37001 externally assessed. Understand the pros and cons for your organisation.

The pros can be very powerful, and don't be daunted by the assessment process itself without compelling reasons.

The assessment

There are at least two UK certification bodies (CBs) that offer ISO 37001 assessments. The best approach, at the time of writing, is to verify with your regular CB that it intends to offer assessment to ISO 37001 in the near future. Organisations that don't have a current CB can inquire with their accreditation body to locate a CB able to assess their ISO 37001 ABMS.

The certification process is the same but there is slightly different terminology for each stage of the assessment.

As ISO 37001 is still a niche assessment product, the initial enquiry will be fielded by a knowledgeable person. They will be pleased to explain the assessment process in detail and the fees involved. Although they will not be able to give consultancy, they could recommend consultants.

If fees and expenses are an important part of the decision, always be sure that you understand the total cost. All CBs quote day rates (a fee for each assessor day), but there may be other costs, such as application fees. Some CBs charge annual management fees, some charge for issuing certificates, and some charge the assessor's travelling expenses and other disbursements. Always get the CB to give you a full breakdown of fees and costs, not just day-rate quotes.

Getting ISO 37001 isn't like passing your driving test. Once you've achieved it, there will be ongoing costs for continuing assessments to maintain the registration. The CB can estimate these costs, for the first three years, at the quotation stage.

The other service you can pay for before deciding on the assessment is for the CB to provide a gap analysis assessment. This is where an ISO 37001 lead assessor (LA) will assess the documented ABMS and then give a written opinion on whether you are ready for the initial assessment process itself.

The gap analysis is usually one or two days but, of course, larger organisations could pay for a longer period. Even a one-day gap analysis will give very useful information about whether you are on the right track with ISO 37001 in terms of meeting external assessment requirements.

The next step is the initial assessment itself, which is typically in two stages: stage 1 looks at the high-level management system that supports the ISO 37001 implementation, and stage 2 looks at how this has been implemented throughout the organisation.

The duration of the assessment is based on headcount, the number of locations under the proposed ISO 37001 certification, and risk factors, such as the location of the business and the business streams themselves. Although there may be some variation in the days the three CBs will quote, essentially they all use the same formula, and it is pointless if you are quoted, say, eight days of assessment, insisting they do it in two. They are regulated businesses with reputations to maintain and income streams to protect. The most important cost is the management time and opportunity cost within your own organisation, so the assessment fees are only one element of the budget.

A lead assessor will be appointed by the CB and they will contact you in advance of the assessment to agree an assessment plan. At the end of each assessment you will receive a report with a recommendation.

An assessment is not an exam with a pass mark. All the requirements of ISO 37001 need to be met, although there may be different levels of maturity for different elements of the system.

The assessment will be a combination of interviews and looking at documentary evidence (both electronic and hard copy). These must be available at the assessment. All the CBs have a confidentiality agreement process, so if there are processes you feel you can't show to the lead assessor, then this needs to be agreed in advance with the CB. It is certainly not a topic for the assessment opening meeting.

The lead assessor is not a client or a prospect – encourage all staff to be candid with them. They are trained to believe what the auditee tells them, until it is tested elsewhere, so prevarication or obfuscation isn't clever commercial negotiation – it can be disastrous for the outcome of an assessment.

Being either adversarial or fawning towards a lead assessor is also counter-productive. A friendly, professional relationship is ideal. If you really feel that you can't work with the lead assessor assigned, then this should be discussed with the CB immediately. Suffering in silence tends to lead to problems later in the assessment process that can be difficult to resolve.

The end game?

The CB might offer you an ISO 37001 certificate at the end of the initial assessment process, or may need you to have further assessment. The assessment recommendation is typically based on the type and number of nonconformities raised. It is important to advise staff in advance that nonconformities are against the process and not them personally!

The point of having an assessment in two stages is that the majority of key issues will – hopefully – be identified at stage 1 and resolved before stage 2.

Once the ISO 37001 certificate is issued, a programme of continuing assessments or surveillance visits is agreed. Nonconformities can be raised at these visits, and every three years a reassessment takes place.

The end game isn't really getting the certificate but maintaining it. Yet that needn't be an imposition. It is an opportunity to develop the system. Use the CB as a sounding board and a resource for your plans and challenges. They can't give consultancy but they can provide added value.

ITG RESOURCES

IT Governance Ltd sources, creates and delivers products and services to meet the real-world, evolving IT governance needs of today's organisations, directors, managers and practitioners.

The ITG website (*www.itgovernance.co.uk*) is the international one-stop-shop for corporate and IT governance information, advice, guidance, books, tools, training and consultancy.

Publishing Services

IT Governance Publishing (ITGP) is the world's leading IT-GRC publishing imprint that is wholly owned by IT Governance Ltd.

With books and tools covering all IT governance, risk and compliance frameworks, we are the publisher of choice for authors and distributors alike, producing unique and practical publications of the highest quality, in the latest formats available, which readers will find invaluable.

www.itgovernancepublishing.co.uk is the website dedicated to ITGP. Other titles published by ITGP that may be of interest include:

- Reviewing IT in Due Diligence
  www.itgovernance.co.uk/shop/product/reviewing-it-in-due-diligence-are-you-buying-an-it-asset-or-liability

- Governance and Internal Controls for Cutting Edge IT
  www.itgovernance.co.uk/shop/product/governance-and-internal-controls-for-cutting-edge-it
- The Case for ISO27001: 2013
  www.itgovernance.co.uk/shop/product/the-case-for-iso-27001-2013-second-edition

We also offer a range of toolkits that provide organisations with comprehensive and customisable documents to help create the specific documentation required to properly implement management systems or standards. Written by experienced practitioners and based on the latest best practice, ITGP toolkits can save months of work for organisations working toward compliance with a given standard.

Of particular interest to readers of this guide will be the ABMS Anti-Bribery Documentation Toolkit:

www.itgovernance.co.uk/shop/product/abms-anti-bribery-documentation-toolkit

To see the full range of toolkits visit
www.itgovernance.co.uk/shop/category/itgp-toolkits

Books and tools published by IT Governance Publishing (ITGP) are available from all business booksellers and the following websites:

www.itgovernance.eu   *www.itgovernanceusa.com*

www.itgovernance.asia   *www.itgovernancesa.co.za*

Training Services

Organisations that are serious about their information security should employ best-practice security practices. Staff training is an essential component of the best-practice information security triad of people, processes and technology. IT Governance's ISO27001 Learning Pathway provides information security courses from Foundation to Advanced level, with qualifications awarded by IBITGQ.

Many courses are available in Live Online as well as classroom formats, so delegates can learn and achieve essential career progression from the comfort of their own homes and offices.

For information on any of our courses, including PCI DSS compliance, business continuity, IT governance, service management and professional certification courses, please see: *www.itgovernance.co.uk/training.aspx*.

Professional Services and Consultancy

The confidentiality, integrity and availability of information is an important aspect of anti-bribery record keeping. Fortunately, an ABMS can be implemented as part of a wider information security management system (ISMS).

ISO27001, the international standard for information security management, sets out the requirements of an ISMS, a holistic approach to information security that encompasses people, process, and technology.

Implementing, maintaining and continually improving an ISMS can be a daunting task. Fortunately, IT Governance's consultants offer a comprehensive range of flexible, practical support packages to help organisations of any size, sector or location to implement an ISMS and achieve certification to ISO27001.

For general information about our consultancy services, including for ISO 27001, ISO 20000, ISO 22301, Cyber Essentials, the PCI DSS, the GDPR and more, please see: *www.itgovernance.co.uk/consulting.aspx*.

Daily Sentinel newsletter

You can stay up to date with the latest developments across the whole spectrum of IT governance subject matter including risk management, information security, ITIL and IT service management, project governance, compliance, and so much more by subscribing to our newsletter.

Simply visit our subscription centre and select your preferences:

www.itgovernance.co.uk/daily-sentinel

EU for product safety is Stephen Evans, The Mill Enterprise Hub, Stagreenan, Drogheda, Co. Louth, A92 CD3D, Ireland. (servicecentre@itgovernance.eu)

www.ingramcontent.com/pod-product-compliance
Lightning Source LLC
Chambersburg PA
CBHW071122210326
41519CB00020B/6393